SUPER CUTE!

Baby

DOGS

by Kari Schuetz

BLASTOFF! READERS

BELLWETHER MEDIA · MINNEAPOLIS, MN

Note to Librarians, Teachers, and Parents:

Blastoff! Readers are carefully developed by literacy experts and combine standards-based content with developmentally appropriate text.

Level 1 provides the most support through repetition of high-frequency words, light text, predictable sentence patterns, and strong visual support.

Level 2 offers early readers a bit more challenge through varied simple sentences, increased text load, and less repetition of high-frequency words.

Level 3 advances early-fluent readers toward fluency through increased text and concept load, less reliance on visuals, longer sentences, and more literary language.

Level 4 builds reading stamina by providing more text per page, increased use of punctuation, greater variation in sentence patterns, and increasingly challenging vocabulary.

Level 5 encourages children to move from "learning to read" to "reading to learn" by providing even more text, varied writing styles, and less familiar topics.

Whichever book is right for your reader, Blastoff! Readers are the perfect books to build confidence and encourage a love of reading that will last a lifetime!

This edition first published in 2014 by Bellwether Media, Inc.

No part of this publication may be reproduced in whole or in part without written permission of the publisher. For information regarding permission, write to Bellwether Media, Inc., Attention: Permissions Department, 5357 Penn Avenue South, Minneapolis, MN 55419.

Library of Congress Cataloging-in-Publication Data

Schuetz, Kari.
 Baby dogs / by Kari Schuetz.
   p. cm. – (Blastoff! readers. Super cute!)
 Audience: K to grade 3.
 Summary: "Developed by literacy experts for students in kindergarten through grade three, this book introduces baby dogs to young readers through leveled text and related photos"– Provided by publisher.
 Includes bibliographical references and index.
 ISBN 978-1-60014-926-9 (hardcover : alk. paper)
 1. Puppies–Juvenile literature. 2. Dogs–Juvenile literature. 3. Animals–Infancy–Juvenile literature. I. Title.
 SF426.5.S338 2014
 636.707–dc23
                                                          2013009637

Printed in the United States of America, North Mankato, MN.

Table of Contents

Puppies!

Young dogs are
called puppies.
Dogs can be
puppies until
age 2.

Puppies are born in **litters**. Big dogs have the largest litters.

Life With the Litter

Young puppies let mom lick them clean.

They drink
mom's milk
together.

Brothers and sisters **wrestle** with one another. They bite and scratch to play.

A New Home

A puppy can leave mom at 8 weeks old. It moves to a new home.

The puppy **bonds** with its owner. It loves belly rubs.

It follows
the owner's
commands.
"Sit" is one
trick it learns.

The puppy
wants to play.
It chews on
toys and sticks.
What a treat!

Glossary

bonds—becomes close

commands—orders to follow

litters—groups of babies born together

wrestle—to fight in a playful way

To Learn More

AT THE LIBRARY

Arlon, Penelope. *Puppies and Kittens.* New York, N.Y.: Scholastic, 2013.

DK Publishing. *See How They Grow: Puppy.* New York, N.Y.: DK Publishing, 2007.

Elora, Grace. *Puppies.* New York, N.Y.: Gareth Stevens Pub., 2011.

ON THE WEB

Learning more about dogs is as easy as 1, 2, 3.

1. Go to www.factsurfer.com.

2. Enter "dogs" into the search box.

3. Click the "Surf" button and you will see a list of related Web sites.

With factsurfer.com, finding more information is just a click away.

Index

The images in this book are reproduced through the courtesy of: Mila Atkovska, front cover; Juan Martinez, pp. 4-5; Minden Pictures/ SuperStock, pp. 6-7; Juniors/ SuperStock, pp. 8-9; Matka_Wariatka, pp. 10-11; Gary Randall/ Kimball Stock, pp. 12-13, 20-21; Tanya Constantine/ Glow Images, pp. 14-15; Photolyric, pp. 16-17; Golden Pixels LLC, pp. 18-19.